MEDITERRANEAN DIET

50 OF THE BEST MEDITERRANEAN DIET RECIPES FOR WEIGHT LOSS

A COOK'S SIMPLE GUIDE AND RECIPE BOOK

EMILY R. STONE

Mediterranean Diet:

50 of the Best Mediterranean Diet Recipes for Weight Loss

A Cook's Simple Guide and Recipe Book

by

Emily R. Stone

Emily R. Stone
Copyright © 2013 Emily R. Stone

TABLE OF CONTENTS

Publisher's Notes.. 8

Dedication 9

Chapter One - The Mediterranean Diet- What is It? 10

Chapter Two - What Are the Overall Benefits of Being on the Mediterranean Diet? 15

Chapter Three - Is The Mediterranean Diet Healthy?...........19

Chapter Four - 10 Mediterranean Diet Breakfast Recipes 23

    Vegetarian Omelet 23

    Breakfast Smoothie 25

    Pancakes with Fruit...26

    Salmon and Asparagus Egg White Omelet 27

    Peanut Butter on Toast or a Bagel............................28

    Oatmeal with Fruit and Nuts 29

    Apricot Halves with Greek Yogurt............................30

    Zucchini and Goat Cheese Frittata...........................31

    Fruit and Yogurt Parfait with Granola 32

    Toast with Fruit and Cheese 33

CHAPTER FIVE - 10 Mediterranean Diet Lunch Recipes 34

    Vegetable Sandwich with Hummus 34

Feta and Artichoke Pizza 35

Berry and Almond Couscous 36

Pasta Fagioli 37

Grilled Chicken Salad 38

Whole Wheat Turkey Wrap 39

Shrimp Pasta 40

Caprese Salad 41

Mediterranean Omelet 42

Tuna Salad with Crackers 43

CHAPTER SIX - 10 Mediterranean Diet Dinner Recipes 44

Mediterranean Wrap 44

Curried Vegetables 46

Tomato and Eggplant Salad 47

Veggie Tofu Stir Fry 48

Grilled Corn and Poblano Salad with Chipotle Vinaigrette
.... 50

Chard Tacos 51

Eggplant Surprise 52

Chicken and Quinoa Salad 53

Mediterranean Kale 55

Vegan Arepas with Polenta 56

Grilled Vegetable Sandwich 58

CHAPTER SEVEN - 10 Mediterranean Diet Gluten-Free Recipes
....59

Cheesy Flat Bread Gluten-Free...59

Grilled Pita Bread Gluten-Free..61

Falafel Balls Gluten-Free 62

Sweet Potato Latkes Gluten-Free..63

Hummus Gluten-Free 64

Baked Pita Chips Gluten-Free 65

Stuffed Pita Pockets Gluten-Free 66

Greek Style Roasted Potatoes Gluten-Free............................67

Grilled Lamb Chops Gluten-Free 68

Tzatziki Gluten-Free 69

CHAPTER EIGHT - 10 Mediterranean Diet Snack/Dessert
Recipes..70

Sangria Granita 70

Crema Di Mascarpone (Chilled Cheese Dessert) 71

Berlingozzo 72

Honey and Tahini Ganache with Toasted Sesame Seeds .73

Poached Cherries..74

Berry Panna Cotta 75

Roasted Figs with Caramel 76

Red Grape, Polenta & Olive Oil Cake 77

Emily R. Stone
Ainse & Fig Ice Cream 78

Red Wine Poached Pear 79

About The Author.. 80

PUBLISHER'S NOTES

Disclaimer

This publication is intended to provide helpful and informative information. It is not intended to diagnose, treat, cure, or prevent any health problem or condition, nor is intended to replace the advice of a physician. No action should be taken solely on the contents of this book. Always consult your physician or qualified health-care professional on any matters regarding your health and before adopting any suggestions in this book or drawing inferences from it.

The author and publisher specifically disclaim all responsibility for any liability, loss or risk, personal or otherwise, which is incurred as a consequence, directly or indirectly, from the use or application of any contents of this book.

Any and all product names referenced within this book are the trademarks of their respective owners. None of these owners have sponsored, authorized, endorsed, or approved this book.

Always read all information provided by the manufacturers' product labels before using their products. The author and publisher are not responsible for claims made by manufacturers.

DEDICATION

To my kids, who inspire me every day in my journey towards healthier eating.

CHAPTER ONE - THE MEDITERRANEAN DIET- WHAT IS IT?

A Mediterranean diet consists of a variety of foods; you can eat certain vegetables, fruits, poultry, lamb, olive oil, dairy, grains, a bit of wine on occasion, and you can also consume fish. You will find that a Mediterranean diet is filled with foods that have unsaturated fats and antioxidants too.

As you check out various meal plans, make sure you really like the recipes offered. If not, you can substitute one acceptable food item for another, provided that the fat and calorie contents are within the diet's guidelines. For example, if a diet plan recommends that you eat peaches and you really don't care for them, you can substitute the peaches for strawberries. If a meal plan offers you a fish recipe and you prefer poultry, that's perfectly fine too. You will find that these plans are highly adaptable for your personal needs and likes.

A Mediterranean diet meal plan includes beverages as well. You can drink water, diet sodas, and diet iced teas. If you want more flavor in the iced teas, you can use fresh lemons to add additional flavoring. Flavored seltzers are also allowed, and all beverages that are calorie free can be consumed when on the Mediterranean Diet plan. It is recommended, however, that you limit your consumption of coffee, tea and other caffeinated beverages to no more than three full cups in a given day. You will also want to cut back on your use of sugar; an appropriate sugar substitute will suffice.

Being healthy and keeping your body fit more often than not means losing weight. You enroll in different exercise programs like dance, aerobics, pilates, kickboxing, and even yoga but nothing seems to work. You shed a few pounds, but after a while you gain them back just as fast as you lost them. And so you go on a diet. You research the hottest diets and decide to follow one. Then you realize that this, too, won't work because it just keeps you starving and wanting more food.

Well, you do not need to worry any longer. There's a diet that can help you lose weight without requiring you to starve. Try the Mediterranean Diet. This way of eating, though, should not be viewed as a diet; it's a lifestyle. For years, people who live around the Mediterranean have used the freshest and finest ingredients when cooking. This has been the inspiration for this so-called diet, as you are encouraged to incorporate only the healthiest foods in every meal.

Basically, the Mediterranean Diet plan is all about eating healthy, including fish and vegetables in your diet and using a lot of olive oil to avoid a large consumption of saturated fats. Your diet should include about 20% protein, 30% healthy fats, and 50%

carbohydrates. These recommended percentages are well balanced to ensure a perfectly working diet.

Here are some simple guidelines for following the Mediterranean Diet plan:

1. Include lots of fruits and vegetables in your diet. Organically grown options are better, because you can be sure they are safe and healthy. Be creative! Turn them into salads, and enjoy them drizzled with olive oil or a vinaigrette.

2. Use a hearty amount of olive oil when cooking. People living in the Mediterranean region are known for recipes that use olive oil instead of butter or lard. This helps moderate your overall fat intake.

3. For carbohydrates, eat pasta or whole grain bread combined with proteins such as fish. You may eat red meat, but only in moderation.

4. When following the Mediterranean Diet plan, remember to drink lots of water throughout the day. You may also pair your meals with a good bottle of wine. Drinking wine, especially red wine, is also recommended as wine has many health benefits.

5. Dairy products like cheese and yogurt should also be used in moderation, as they may increase the amount of fat in your diet.

6. Use honey instead of sugar as a sweetener.

Since the Mediterranean Diet plan is not about starving yourself, it is important that you eat meals three times a day and small, healthy snacks whenever you feel hungry. This diet plan will be successful if you follow it continuously. Don't think of it as a diet you'll start and eventually complete. Make it your regular eating habit from this point forward. You will be able to maintain your weight while staying healthy at the same time.

The remarkable health of the people from the Mediterranean region has always been a wonder to researchers. The people in the Mediterranean region are known to have a very active lifestyle. Of course, physical activity is essential for good health, but good health is based on good food habits as well. In other words, the Mediterranean diet is a healthy diet rich in plant food - especially whole grains, cereals, vegetables, fruit, nuts, legumes and olives. All ensure good health and a lower chance of developing heart disease.

The Mediterranean Diet includes all types of foods that are recommended on a normal, low to moderate basis. This method is explained by the traditional Mediterranean Diet pyramid. The pyramid classifies various foods depending on their nutritional value, and indicates whether a food is to be eaten daily, a few days a week or only a few times per month.

Food that can be consumed on a day-to-day basis includes cereals, vegetables, bread, beans, potatoes, leafy vegetables and other plant products. Interestingly, nuts rich in essential fatty acids, vitamins and minerals are also included in the daily diet. The diet does not recommend very much processing of food, as doing so can easily deplete nutritional values. For instance, over-cooked vegetables are only good as roughage (they contain fiber), because they lose essential vitamins in the cooking process. Food should be cooked, garnished or dressed in olive oil, a rich source of low saturated fat. Consumed moderately, it is known to play a vital role in preventing heart disease.

Milk and milk products such as cheese and yogurt are consumed daily on a low to moderate basis. But butter, high in saturated fat, is a total no-no on the Mediterranean Diet's recommended food list. Wine is allowed daily on a moderate basis.

Food from animals, especially chicken, eggs, and seafood, is allowed weekly on the Mediterranean Diet. For instance, eggs are consumed four days a week. But red meat, high in saturated fat, is allowed only a few times per month. The diet recommends veal and lamb instead of beef because their fat content is comparatively lower than that of beef. Meat should be trimmed of visible fat and is often roasted or grilled. Sweets and desserts are also a part of the weekly diet. The most preferred dessert is fruit.

Food on the Mediterranean Diet provides fiber (mainly from vegetables and fruit), good fat (olive oil), nutrients, vitamins, minerals, proteins, and essential acids necessary for a human body to stay fit and healthy.

CHAPTER TWO - WHAT ARE THE OVERALL BENEFITS OF BEING ON THE MEDITERRANEAN DIET?

Because of extensive research on eating habits and their connection to healthy living, and the fact more people are seeking to live a healthier lifestyle, dieting is more popular than ever. While anyone can find a diet plan that fits his or her needs, none have proven to be as effective as the Mediterranean Diet. While the health benefits that come with the Mediterranean Diet are vast, the number one benefit is found in the overall heart health associated with it. Many diet plans have incorporated some components of the Mediterranean Diet, but the foundation of the Mediterranean Diet has not changed.

When looking at the health benefits of following a Mediterranean Diet, health and wellness experts point to research that shows people who follow the diet enjoy less risk of heart disease, death associated with heart disease, and a lower risk of being diagnosed with cancer. Following the Mediterranean Diet is also linked to a reduction in the risk of getting Alzheimer's and Parkinson's disease. Less research has been conducted, but supporters of the Mediterranean Diet plan also boast of increased vitality, a more youthful existence, and an overall improvement in their health.

The Mediterranean Diet operates on the belief that any successful diet must emphasize several steps to a healthy heart, including lowering the intake of unhealthy fats, while increasing the intake of fruits and vegetables, whole grains, and fish. Unhealthy oils are replaced with healthier choices like olive oil. Portion sizes are also important when following the Mediterranean Diet, along with substituting healthy, flavorful herbs and spices instead of salt, which increases the risk of hypertension. Followers of the Mediterranean Diet are encouraged to eat red meat in strict moderation, but are allowed to incorporate a glass of red wine on occasion into their diet.

The Mediterranean region, where the foundation of the diet was established, is well known for healthy eating habits. Many people of Mediterranean decent are known for eating six or more servings of fruits and vegetables every day. Whole grains are also very popular on this diet plan, and the focus is placed on using grains without unhealthy trans-fats. The diet also allows followers to include bread in their diet, but substitute olive oil for unhealthy butter and margarine. Many people who follow the diet eat their bread plain, but some dip the bread in olive oil for added flavor.

Another variation of the Mediterranean Diet is the inclusion of nuts. While nuts are known for having high fat content, the fat found in most nuts is considered healthy by dietary experts. Because of the high fat content, followers of the diet are instructed to eat nuts in moderation, limiting themselves to about one handful per day or less. People who enjoy eating nuts are encouraged to select nuts with less salt, and nuts that are not honey-roasted or candied. Peanut oil and other oils derived from nuts are considered a better choice than oils full of saturated fat and trans-fat.

Another known benefit of following the Mediterranean Diet is the inclusion of foods high in healthy omega-3 fatty acids. Dietary experts emphasize that omega-3 fatty acids are associated with a decrease in the risk of sudden heart attacks, and are believed to help regulate blood pressure. Such fatty fish, including sardines, mackerel, salmon, and albacore tuna, are great sources of omega-3 fatty acids and can be eaten daily on the Mediterranean Diet plan. Followers of the diet are encouraged to make fish a daily selection in order to enjoy decreased risk of blood clots, and to increase the overall blood vessel health associated with diets high in omega-3 fatty acids.

One of the biggest drawbacks to most diet plans is not enjoying the food you are allowed to eat, and having limited choices, which eventually leads to boredom and burn out. A great benefit of the Mediterranean Diet is the delicious variety of foods allowed and encouraged, as well as the overall enjoyment of the Mediterranean style of preparing dishes. By incorporating a wide variety of fruits in vegetables, dieters reduce the risk of becoming tired of the same menu each day. The Mediterranean Diet encourages followers to eat fruit salads, fresh fruits and vegetables as snacks, and to prepare them in a wide variety of methods including boiling, baking, and grilling. Fruits and vegetables are often added to casseroles and other dishes, for instance.

Most Mediterranean Diet plans allow for a moderate amount of wine consumption. While dieters are cautioned about the calories in alcohol, followers of the Mediterranean Diet are allowed to include five to ten ounces of wine in their daily diet. There has been a lot of debate regarding the health benefits of wine in recent years, but most medical experts believe wine consumed in strict moderation is associated with lower risks of heart disease. Too much alcohol consumption is associated with a variety of health and wellness risks.

The benefits of the Mediterranean Diet are impressive. People who have chosen to follow the Mediterranean Diet boast about the documented health benefits. They also point out that the diet allows for such a tasty variety of food, they rarely burn out or become bored with the diet. Anyone who is looking to improve their heart health or to lose unwanted pounds is encouraged to try the Mediterranean Diet. No other diet offers such great health benefits, while also providing a wide range of allowable foods that are enjoyed by millions all over the world.

CHAPTER THREE - IS THE MEDITERRANEAN DIET HEALTHY?

The Mediterranean Diet is a diet recommended by many doctors. In fact, the renowned Mayo Clinic has popularized the diet for its health benefits. Those who don't understand how the Mediterranean Diet works may wonder if it really is healthy. The answer is quite simply, yes! There are many reasons why the Mediterranean Diet is considered to be one of the healthiest diets. Compared to the traditional Western diet, the Mediterranean Diet offers significantly more health benefits to those that choose to follow the regimen. Let's examine these more closely.

Why the Western Diet Is Bad For Health

The typical American diet is basically a heart attack waiting to happen. Quite often, Americans become caught up in their everyday work life and, as a result, choose to eat meals that are quick and ready to go. In the morning, breakfast will often consist of sugary cereal that has a lot of additives and preservatives and, unfortunately, chemically treated milk. Lunch is usually some type of Fast Food that is loaded with saturated fat, salt, additives and preservatives. Dinner is quite possibly the only meal of the day that actually has a hint of nutrition. Furthermore, the beverage of choice for many Americans is soda, and snacks like chips and candy bars tend to have little nutritional value. In some cases, they even deplete the body of its nutrients!

Why the Mediterranean Diet Is Good For Health

There are many reasons why the Mediterranean Diet is a far superior option for good health. There are a few basic eating habits that promote good health; they consist of eating primarily fruits and vegetables, fish and whole grains, and eliminating unhealthy fats and sugars. Plus, because many such foods are naturally low in calories, losing weight becomes a very natural process. These are all things we should do to maintain good health, but many diets just do not have all these components.

The Mediterranean Diet is ideal because it focuses on whole foods while eliminating the additives and preservatives that are usually found in the traditional American diet. On the Mediterranean Diet, food is usually prepared at home from scratch using natural ingredients. Fats used for cooking are healthy fats. Olive oil is used not only for cooking meals, but as flavor enhancers on vegetables, pasta and bread. Since olive trees are native to the Mediterranean region, olive oil is easily accessible and enjoyed even in its most basic state.

The people of the Mediterranean are well known for their delicious salads. Salads are typically eaten with both lunch and dinner. They usually include fresh vegetables such as lettuce, tomatoes, olives, onions and things of the like. A typical Greek, Turkish or Italian salad also usually includes some type of delicious cheese. While those living in the Mediterranean region do enjoy eating cheese, they eat it in moderation and sparingly with meals.

Nuts are also a big part of the Mediterranean Diet even though they are high in fat; they're simply eaten in small amounts. In order to get the true benefit of nuts, they should be eaten raw or slightly toasted.

Research regarding the traditional Mediterranean diet has shown it can also help lower cholesterol, in addition to its other health benefits. Since there have been so many studies done proving that the Mediterranean Diet is beneficial for health, it is a wonderful idea to think about implementing this diet for your family's all-around good health. The weight loss you're likely to experience is, of course, an added benefit.

How to Implement the Mediterranean Diet in Your Life

Nuts are a big part of the Mediterranean Diet. They are great sources of protein, fiber and healthy fats. Keep nuts such as almonds and pistachios close by for a quick healthy snack. Since they are high in calories, it is best to eat them in moderation.

Start substituting healthy fats and oils for butter and margarine. Olive oil can be drizzled over cooked vegetables, salads and bread. When cooking, try to sauté in olive oil instead of canola or vegetable oil. Consider tossing pasta with olive oil and adding garlic and onions.

When it comes to spices, follow the Mediterranean Diet by avoiding a lot of salt. Instead, substitute fresh herbs and spices to give your food delicious flavor.

Follow the Mediterranean Diet when it comes to choosing protein and cut down on red meat. Lamb and poultry are good alternatives, as is fish. In fact, try to eat healthy fish at least three times a week. There are many different varieties of fish, and they offer great benefits to the body and the heart. In particular, look for cold-water fish like salmon or mackerel that are loaded with omega-3 fatty acids. When preparing fish, focus on baking or grilling methods instead of frying.

These are just some small changes that can be made to the traditional American diet that can help improve your overall health and encourage weight loss. Those following the Mediterranean Diet have fewer problems with heart disease, high cholesterol, and high blood pressure because of what they choose to eat. By avoiding processed foods, saturated fat, and sugar, they find weight loss and weight maintenance comes easily. They also make mealtime a social event, preferring to eat leisurely while surrounded by friends and loved ones. Being around people you love promotes healthy lifestyle.

These changes are all very small, and they are not that difficult to implement. Even though it may seem, at times, to take a lot of work and dedication to follow the Mediterranean Diet, the benefits the diet will bring to a family's overall health make it worthwhile to give it a try.

CHAPTER FOUR - 10 MEDITERRANEAN DIET BREAKFAST RECIPES

People are growing ever more health-conscious with each passing day, and there is an increasing focus on diet and eating healthy. Following the Mediterranean Diet involves avoiding unhealthy fats, such as butter, while consuming fruits, vegetables, whole grains, legumes, and fish. As a result, it lends itself naturally to weight loss. This diet promotes heart health and helps prevent high blood pressure and high cholesterol levels. Eating on the Mediterranean Diet is not difficult, but it does require awareness of things that should be avoided like fatty proteins, butter and margarine, processed foods and sugar. The focus on this diet is not to avoid fat or carbohydrates, but to consume healthy ones. Here are some quick and simple breakfast recipes for followers of this diet.

VEGETARIAN OMELET

Eggs are a wonderful protein source and are utilized in many Mediterranean Diets. Omelets are easy to prepare and cook. A large variety of vegetables, including broccoli, peppers, and asparagus, can be added to whole eggs or egg whites before cooking. This breakfast is fun and can be easily adjusted for personal taste with the addition of herbs, vegetables, spices, and cheese.

Ingredients:

2-3 eggs or egg whites
Broccoli
Peppers
Asparagus
Salt and pepper
Cheese (optional)

Directions:

Use 2-3 eggs or egg whites for a single omelet, and add the vegetables and other ingredients during the cooking process. Some vegetables may require cooking prior to being added to a cooking omelet. Cheese, while not always a healthy option, can make this meal unforgettable.

Emily R. Stone
BREAKFAST SMOOTHIE

Ingredients:

Berries (strawberries, blackberries, raspberries, and blueberries)
Bananas
Fruit juice
Ice cubes
Pomegranate (optional)
Apple juice (optional)

Directions:

This smoothie is healthy, cool, and sweet. Combine berries, bananas, fruit juice, flaxseed, and 5-6 ice cubes in a blender. While strawberries, blackberries, raspberries, and blueberries are most commonly used, other berries or fruits can be substituted. The fruit juice can also be adjusted, but pomegranate and apple juice, add a kick to the smoothie. Blend all of the ingredients until they are smooth and serve in a tall glass.

PANCAKES WITH FRUIT

Ingredients:

1½ cups low fat yogurt
1 cup whole wheat flour
¾ cup fat free milk
1 egg

Optional:

Bananas
Berries
Syrup

Directions:

Pancakes made with whole-wheat flour and yogurt are a fluffy and delicious Mediterranean breakfast. Mix 1 and 1/2 cup low-fat yogurt with 1 cup whole-wheat flour, 1 egg, and 3/4 cup fat-free milk to make 20 small pancakes. Extras can be frozen for later consumption. Adding a favorite fruit, such as bananas or berries, can add a juicy flavor to the pancakes, and syrup is often forgone.

Emily R. Stone
SALMON AND ASPARAGUS EGG WHITE OMELET

Ingredients:

2-3 egg whites

Asparagus
Salmon (chopped)
Pepper
Chives
Rosemary
Parsley
Lemon juice

Directions:

An omelet made of egg whites, salmon, and asparagus promotes heart health and has a unique flavor. Using 2 or 3 egg whites, mix in chopped salmon and asparagus before cooking. Parsley, rosemary, chives, and pepper can be used for additional seasoning of the omelets. Add lemon juice to contrast the flavor of the fish during the cooking process.

PEANUT BUTTER ON TOAST OR A BAGEL

Ingredients:

Whole wheat bagels
Peanut butter
Grapes

Directions:

Whole-wheat bagels are an easy, quick breakfast for those following the Mediterranean Diet. Peanut butter provides healthy protein, and when 3 tablespoons are spread on a whole-wheat bagel, it provides a filling breakfast. Add a side of grapes or similar fruit for additional flavor and texture to the meal. This breakfast is ideal for the person on the go who does not want to sacrifice the dietary choices they make for the sake of speed.

Emily R. Stone
OATMEAL WITH FRUIT AND NUTS

Ingredients:

Oatmeal
Cinnamon
Apples
Raisins
Dried cranberries
Nuts (assorted)

Directions:

Prepare oatmeal as per instruction and add the rest of the ingredients. Oatmeal can be easy to make and may seem overly simple, but it is hardly the boring breakfast that memory portrays it as. Adding a variety of fruits, nuts, and spices can certainly build an amazing breakfast.

Apples, walnuts, and cinnamon make a great autumn favorite. Raisins and dried cranberries can be added to oatmeal for a classic taste. Blueberries, strawberries, and bananas can be added to oatmeal for a fruity and festive breakfast. This breakfast is often seasonal, as the fruits available during various parts of the year differ.

APRICOT HALVES WITH GREEK YOGURT

Ingredients:

Apricot (cut in halves)
Greek yogurt
Granola
Honey

Directions:

A traditional Mediterranean breakfast is an apricot sliced in half with Greek yogurt on each half. It is then drizzled with honey or granola for additional flavor or texture. This breakfast is light and sweet, and provides a lot of energy for the day. Additional fruits or nuts can be used to top this breakfast as well, allowing for a great deal of individuality in this meal. Serving this meal with a cold drink, such as low-fat strawberry or chocolate milk, is ideal.

Emily R. Stone
ZUCCHINI AND GOAT CHEESE FRITTATA

Ingredients:

2 medium sliced zucchinis
8 eggs
2 tablespoons low-fat milk
1/8 teaspoon pepper
1/4 teaspoon salt
1 tablespoon olive oil
1 crushed clove garlic
2 ounces of goat cheese

Directions:

A common Italian breakfast, this meal takes more time to prepare. Slice the zucchinis and cook them in a cast-iron skillet in the olive oil and garlic mixture. When this has cooked for 5 minutes, pour the mixture of milk, eggs, salt, and pepper over it. Finally, add the goat cheese to the top. Place the skillet in the oven for 12 minutes, and then allow it to sit for 3 additional minutes before cutting and serving the frittata.

FRUIT AND YOGURT PARFAIT WITH GRANOLA

Ingredients:

Low fat yogurt
Granola
Fruit of choice
Pecans
Walnuts

Directions:

Mixing low-fat yogurt with fruit and granola is the ideal easy breakfast for the Mediterranean Diet. Any fruit can be added to taste, though the most popular fruits included are generally strawberries, blueberries, and raspberries. The granola adds a crunch to the meal, and may also be available in flavored varieties that include different components. Nuts such as walnuts or pecans can be added for flavor and the addition of a healthy fat to the meal.

Emily R. Stone
TOAST WITH FRUIT AND CHEESE

Ingredients:

Toast
Fruit (strawberries, raspberries or blueberries)
Cheese slices
Peanut butter (optional)

Directions:

The combination of fruit and cheese is a classic Mediterranean choice, and combining these with a whole-wheat toast creates a breakfast that is healthy and cannot be eaten too quickly. The food is appreciated, as it is in Mediterranean countries, because it is not consumed at a rapid pace. Toast, with or without a bit of peanut butter spread, can be eaten with sliced cheese and fruit on top or on the side, and this breakfast often serves as a social one for the family following a Mediterranean Diet.

CHAPTER FIVE - 10 MEDITERRANEAN DIET LUNCH RECIPES

VEGETABLE SANDWICH WITH HUMMUS

Ingredients:

2 tbsp sun dried tomato hummus
2 slices whole grain bread
1/4 c baby spinach leaves
2 slices of yellow pepper
2 slices of tomato
1 tbsp sliced black olives
1 tsp olive oil for drizzling
Handful of alfalfa sprouts
Pepper and Salt to taste

Directions:

Spread 1 tablespoon of hummus on each slice of bread. Layer the spinach leaves, pepper, tomato, olives, and alfalfa sprouts on one slice of bread. Drizzle the vegetables with olive oil and sprinkle with pepper and salt. Top with the remaining bread slice.

Emily R. Stone
FETA AND ARTICHOKE PIZZA

Ingredients:

1 8-inch whole wheat prepared pizza crust
1/4 c feta cheese
1 tomato, thinly sliced
1/4 c artichoke hearts packed in olive oil, drained and chopped
1/4 c black olives
1 tbsp garlic-flavored olive oil
1 tsp dried Italian seasoning

Directions:

Sprinkle the feta cheese over the prepared pizza crust. Arrange the sliced tomato, artichoke hearts, and olives evenly over the cheese. Drizzle the garlic-flavored olive oil over the top of the vegetables and sprinkle with the Italian seasoning. Bake in a preheated 425 degree oven for 8 to 10 minutes.

BERRY AND ALMOND COUSCOUS

Ingredients:

1 c whole-wheat couscous, cooked and cooled to room temperature
2 tbsp olive oil
2 tbsp apple cider vinegar
1/4 c strawberries, sliced
1/4 c blueberries
2 tbsp sliced almonds, toasted
Salt and pepper to taste

Directions:

In a large bowl, whisk the olive oil and vinegar together. Stir in the couscous, strawberries, blueberries, almonds, salt, and pepper until well combined.

Emily R. Stone
Pasta Fagioli

Ingredients:

2 carrots, peeled and diced
2 stalks of celery, diced
1/2 white onion, diced
8 oz chicken broth
4 oz tomato sauce
8 oz can cannellini beans
1/4 c whole wheat pasta
1 tsp Italian seasoning
1 tsp garlic powder
1/4 tsp salt and pepper
1 tbsp olive oil

Directions:

In a medium sauce pot, sauté the carrots, celery, and onion in olive oil until softened. Stir in chicken broth, tomato sauce, cannellini beans, Italian seasoning, garlic powder, salt, and pepper. Simmer for 10 minutes. Stir in pasta and cook another 10 minutes or until pasta is tender.

GRILLED CHICKEN SALAD

Ingredients:

1 boneless, skinless chicken breast, grilled
2 c baby spinach leaves
1/2 avocado, sliced
1/4 c cucumber, sliced
1/2 roma tomato, diced
1/4 c kalamata olives
2 tbsp vinegar (red wine)
2 tbsp olive oil
1/2 tsp Italian seasoning
Pepper and Salt to taste

Directions:

Whisk the red wine vinegar, olive oil, Italian seasoning, pepper and salt in a bowl and set aside. On a plate, layer the spinach leaves, avocado, cucumber, tomato, olives, and sliced chicken breast. Drizzle with the dressing.

Emily R. Stone
WHOLE WHEAT TURKEY WRAP

Ingredients:

1 whole wheat tortilla
2 slices turkey lunch meat
1/4 c salad greens
1/2 avocado, sliced
1/2 roma tomato, sliced
1 tbsp roasted red pepper hummus
1 tsp olive oil

Directions:

Spread a thin layer of hummus onto the whole wheat tortilla. Layer the turkey, salad greens, avocado, and tomato. Drizzle with olive oil and roll into a wrap.

SHRIMP PASTA

Ingredients:

8 oz whole wheat spaghetti, cooked and drained
1 lb shrimp, peeled and deveined
1/2 c cherry tomatoes, halved
1/4 c feta cheese
1 tsp Italian seasoning
2 tbsp garlic-flavored olive oil

Directions:

Sauté shrimp in olive oil until pink and then add in cherry tomatoes and Italian seasoning and cook for 2 minutes to warm tomatoes through. Toss the pasta and feta cheese with the shrimp and tomatoes.

Emily R. Stone
CAPRESE SALAD

Ingredients:

4 slices of fresh mozzarella
4 slices of tomato
8 basil leaves
1 tbsp garlic-flavored olive oil
1/4 tsp dried oregano
Salt and pepper to taste

Directions:

On a plate, alternate the mozzarella, tomato slices, and basil leaves to form a row. Drizzle with the garlic-flavored olive oil and sprinkle with oregano, salt, and pepper.

MEDITERRANEAN OMELET

Ingredients:

1/2 c egg substitute
2 tbsp red pepper, chopped
2 tbsp artichoke hearts, chopped
2 tbsp baby spinach, chopped
2 tbsp tomato, chopped
1 tbsp olive oil
1/4 tsp salt and pepper

Directions:

In a medium skillet, sauté red pepper, artichoke, spinach, tomato, salt, and pepper in the olive oil until softened. Pour in the egg substitute and cook until it is completely set.

Emily R. Stone
TUNA SALAD WITH CRACKERS

Ingredients:

3 oz can tuna packed in water, drained
1/4 c red onion, chopped
1/4 c celery, chopped
1 tbsp Dijon mustard
1 tsp freshly squeezed lemon juice
1 tbsp olive oil
Pepper and Salt to taste
Whole wheat crackers

Directions:

Whisk together the olive oil, Dijon mustard, lemon juice, pepper and salt in a small bowl. Toss the tuna, red onion, and celery together with the dressing. Serve with whole wheat crackers.

CHAPTER SIX - 10 MEDITERRANEAN DIET DINNER RECIPES

MEDITERRANEAN WRAP

Ingredients:

1 sliced onion
1 sliced zucchini
1 sliced eggplant
¼ pound of fresh mushrooms
1 sliced bell pepper
1tbsp of olive oil
¼ cup of goat cheese
¼ cup of basil pesto
4 tortillas
1 sliced avocado
Salt and pepper

Directions:

The preparation time takes about 25 minutes, the cook time is about 10 minutes, the time from start to finish is about 35 minutes and the serving size is 4. Put the bell pepper, mushrooms, eggplant, zucchini and onions in a big container that can be sealed. Add a bit of olive oil to the vegetables and use pepper and salt to season. Cover the container with the lid and shake it to coat.

Heat a skillet or pan over a medium flame then add the vegetables and let cook for approximately ten minutes (until vegetables are tender). Spread a tablespoon of pesto and a tablespoon goat cheese on each tortilla and then add the sliced avocado and then place the veggies on top. Fold the tortillas to make the wrap.

CURRIED VEGETABLES

Ingredients:

3 tbsp of olive oil
1 tbsp powdered curry
½ tsp cumin seeds
1 cubed eggplant
3 seeded jalapeno peppers
4 cubed potatoes
3 sliced tomatoes
½ tsp salt
½ tsp powdered chili
½ tsp ground turmeric
¼ cup of chopped cilantro

Directions:

The preparation time is about 20 minutes, the cook time is about 45 minutes, the time from start to finish is about a hour and 5 minutes and the serving size is 6.

Heat a large pot or Dutch oven over medium heat. Heat the oil, cumin and curry powder until there is an aromatic smell. Mix in turmeric, chili powder, salt, tomatoes, potatoes, jalapenos and eggplant then cover and let cook for approximately forty five minutes. Keep adding water as needed to keep a stew like consistency.

Before serving, sprinkle with cilantro.

Emily R. Stone
TOMATO AND EGGPLANT SALAD

Ingredients:

1 bell pepper
7 tomatoes
1 red pepper
1 eggplant
4 garlic cloves
2 tbsp of tomato paste
¼ cup of olive oil
½ tsp of salt
½ tsp of black pepper
½ tsp of cayenne pepper

Directions:

The preparation time is about 20 minutes, the cook time is about an hour, the time from start to finish is about a hour and 30 minutes and the serving size is between 4 and 6. Roast the red peppers under an oven broiler or on a stove burner until the skin is black then put them in a plastic bag to cool.

To prepare the tomatoes, cut an X on the bottom of each and place in water to boil for about a minute and immediately plunge in cold water to let cool. Cut the eggplant into tiny strips and let sauté in the oil until the eggplant starts to turn brown. Add garlic as soon as the eggplant is soft.

Use cold water to rinse the peppers and take off the burnt skin (ash). Remove the seeds from the peppers and then cut them into small strips and add it to the eggplant. Take the tomatoes, peel them, chop them and add them to the salad. Put in cayenne, pepper, salt and tomato paste. Let boil then lower heat and let simmer for half an hour.

VEGGIE TOFU STIR FRY

Ingredients:

3 tbsp of cornstarch
14 ounce can of vegetable broth
⅓ cup of water
1 minced garlic clove
½ tsp of onion salt
½ tsp black pepper (ground)
½ tsp dry thyme
½ tsp dry basil
½ sp dry parsley
2 tbsp vegetable oil
½ cup of sliced carrots
1 cup of chopped red peppers
1 cup of broccoli
½ cup of trimmed/cut snow peas
12 ounce diced tofu
8 ounces of sliced mushrooms
8 ounce can of corn

Directions:

The preparation time is about 15 minutes, the cook time is about 10 minutes, the time from start to finish is about 25 minutes and the serving size is 4. Add cornstarch to the water and whisk until smooth then combine in a saucepan with parsley, basil, thyme, black pepper, onion salt, garlic and vegetable broth. Let come to a simmer then let cook until gravy is thick (approximately five minutes).

Heat the vegetable oil in a wok or skillet and stir fry the snow peas, broccoli, red pepper and the carrot until they are tender. Add the baby corn, mushrooms and tofu and let cook for another minute. Pour gravy over tofu and vegetables and mix before serving.

GRILLED CORN AND POBLANO SALAD WITH CHIPOTLE VINAIGRETTE

Ingredients:

3 ears of corn
3 tbsp of olive oil
1 pepper (poblano chili)
2 juiced limes
1 chopped chipotle pepper in adobo sauce
½ tsp of salt
1 peeled/pitted/ and chunked avocado
½ cup of chopped cilantro
½ cup of sliced onion

Directions:

The preparation time is about 20 minutes, the cook time is about 15 minutes, the time from start to finish is about 35 minutes and the serving size is 3 1/2 cups. Preheat the outdoor grill and oil the grate lightly. Cook the corn for approximately twenty minutes (turn corn often) and then put aside to cool. Cut the kernels and put them in a large bowl.

Put the poblano chili on the grill to cook until the skin is black then put aside to cool. Peel the poblano chili and remove the seeds then cut the chili into pieces half an inch thick and place in the bowl with the corn.

Whisk salt, chipotle pepper, lime juice and olive oil in a bowl and pour the mixture over the poblano and corn mixture. Put in red onion, cilantro and avocado and toss lightly to coat.

Emily R. Stone
CHARD TACOS

Ingredients:

½ cup of chicken broth
1 quarter inch cut onion
3 minced garlic cloves
1½ tbsp of olive oil
1 tbsp of red pepper flakes
1 bundle of cut and no stemmed Swiss chard
1 tsp salt
1 cup of cheese
12 tortillas
3 quarter cups of salsa

Directions:

The preparation time is about 20 minutes, the cook time is about 45 minutes, the time from start to finish is about a hour and 5 minutes and the serving size is 4. Put some oil in a skillet and heat over medium flame. Add the onion and stir until the onion turns golden brown and is softened.

Put in the red pepper flakes and garlic and mix for about a minute then add the salt, Swiss chard and chicken broth, stir to combine and then cover pan and turn down the heat. Let simmer until the chard is almost tender then take the lid off and turn up the heat to let the liquid evaporate. This should take about five minutes. Take pan off heat and set aside.

Heat another skillet and warm the tortillas then add the chard to the tortilla and put on the salsa and queso fresco cheese topping.

EGGPLANT SURPRISE

Ingredients:

½ teaspoon basil (dried)
1 clove minced garlic
½ cup water
1 ½ tablespoons tomato paste
1 package sliced mushrooms
½ small yellow onion (chopped)
2 small diced zucchini
1 medium peeled and cubed eggplant
Pepper and salt to taste

Directions:

The preparation time is about 10 minutes, the cook time is 45 minutes, the time from start to finish is about 1 hour and the serving size is 2. Preheat oven to 450 degrees Fahrenheit.

Put mushrooms, onion, zucchini and eggplant in a casserole dish (2 quart). Mix water and tomato paste in a tiny bowl then mix in pepper, salt, basil and garlic. Pour mixture over the vegetables and mix thoroughly.

Place in oven to bake until the eggplant is tender (approximately forty five minutes). Put in water if needed. The vegetables should have edges that are slightly browned and be a bit dry.

Emily R. Stone
CHICKEN AND QUINOA SALAD

Ingredients:

2 cups of water
2 cubes of chicken bouillon
1 smashed garlic clove
2 cups of water
1 cup of raw quinoa
2 cooked chicken breasts cut into bite sizes
1 diced onion
1 diced green bell pepper
½ cup of chopped olives
½ cup of feta cheese
¼ cup of parsley (chopped)
¼ cup of chives (chopped)
½ tsp of salt
⅔ cups of lemon juice
½ cup of crumbled feta
1 tablespoon of balsamic vinegar
1/4 cup of olive oil

Directions:

The preparation time is about 15 minutes, the cook time is 20 minutes, the time from start to finish is 35 minutes and the serving size is 4 cups. Use a saucepan and bring water, garlic and bouillon cubes to a boil. Mix in quinoa and turn the heat down then cover the saucepan and let simmer for approximately twenty minutes (until quinoa is soft and all the water is gone). Take out the clove of garlic and place quinoa in a big bowl.

Mix in the chicken, salt, chives, parsley, feta cheese, olives, bell pepper and onion with the quinoa. Drizzle with olive oil, balsamic vinegar and lemon juice and stir to combine. It can be served immediately or placed in refrigerator and served cold.

Emily R. Stone
MEDITERRANEAN KALE

Ingredients:

2 tbsp of lemon juice
12 cups of chopped kale
1 tbsp of minced garlic
1 tsp of soy sauce
1 tbsp of olive oil
Pepper and salt to taste

Directions:

The preparation time is about 15 minutes, the cook time is about 10 minutes, the time from start to finish is about 25 minutes and the serving size is 6. Get a saucepan and put in a steamer insert then fill the pan with water (not more than the bottom of the steamer. Cover and let water come to a boil over a high flame. Put in the kale, cover the pot and let steam until tender (approximately 7 minutes).

Whisk black pepper, salt, soy sauce, garlic, olive oil and lemon juice in a huge bowl. Add dressing to kale and toss to coat.

VEGAN AREPAS WITH POLENTA

Ingredients:

8 ounces of drained tofu
16 ounces polenta
Olive oil
2 sliced bananas
1 cup of black beans
2 peeled/pitted/sliced avocados
1 peeled/seeded/diced mango
¼ cup of diced onions
1 seeded and minced jalapeno pepper
Salt to taste

Directions:

The preparation time is about 20 minutes, the cook time is about 15 minutes, the time from start to finish is about 35 minutes and the serving size is 4 arepas. Preheat the broiler and place the oven rack approximately six inches from source of heat. Also grease the baking sheet.

Cut the polenta and tofu into slabs and place on baking sheet after brushing with olive oil. Cook the polenta and tofu under the broiler until the tops are nice and crispy then take sheet from the oven and place it to one side.

In a skillet, heat some olive oil over medium heat and cook the bananas until they are crispy outside. Each should still be soft on the inside, then take the bananas out and put to one side. Put the black beans in the blender and blend until a sauce is created.

Mix in the salt, jalapeno pepper, diced onion and mango in a bowl. To make the arepas, set out the plates and put polenta on each then add some of the bean sauce, tofu, some bananas, avocado and top with mango salsa.

GRILLED VEGETABLE SANDWICH

Ingredients:

1 sliced eggplant
2 tbsp of olive oil
2 red bell peppers
4 tbsp of mayonnaise
2 sliced mushrooms (Portobello)
3 crushed garlic cloves
1 pound of focaccia bread

Directions:

The preparation time is 20 minutes, the cook time is 40 minutes, the time from start to finish is 3 hours and the serving size is 6. Preheat the oven to four hundred degrees Fahrenheit. Brush the red bell peppers and eggplant with some olive oil. When done place them on the baking sheet and put to roast in the oven for approximately twenty five minutes. Let peppers roast until they are black. Take them out of the oven and let cool.

Heat approximately one tablespoon olive oil then add mushrooms and stir until tender. In the mayonnaise put the crushed garlic. Cut focaccia in half and spread the mayo mix on either half.

Get the peppers and peel them, then remove seeds and slice. Place the mushrooms, peppers and eggplant on the focaccia. Use plastic wrap to wrap sandwich then put a cutting board on it and use some canned foods to add weight; let sit for about two hours before slicing the sandwich and serving.

CHAPTER SEVEN - 10
MEDITERRANEAN DIET GLUTEN-FREE RECIPES

Are you looking for a gluten-free way to enjoy your favorite Mediterranean meals? These 10 Mediterranean recipes will help you enjoy your favorite Mediterranean meals, gluten-free.

CHEESY FLAT BREAD GLUTEN-FREE

Ingredients:

2 tsp active dry yeast
1 tsp sugar
3/4 cups warm water
1 1/4 cups gluten free all purpose baking flour
2 tsp xanthan gum
1/2 tsp salt
1 Tbsp olive oil
1 egg
1 cup shredded mozzarella, Parmesan, and provolone cheese
1 Tbsp garlic powder
1 Tbsp Italian seasonings

Directions:

Combine yeast, sugar, and water in a bowl. Let stand 5 minutes. In a separate bowl, combine flour, xanthan gum, salt, garlic powder, and seasonings. Mix. Add the yeast mixture, egg, and oil. Mix for two minutes on medium speed, periodically scraping down the bowl. With wet hands, shape dough into a ball. Place dough in a bowl. Cover and set in a warm place. Let rise for 30-45 minutes.

Preheat oven to 425 degrees. Wet hands then spread dough evenly onto a pizza pan. Brush dough with olive oil. Bake for 8-10 minutes, until warm.

Remove dough from oven. Top with cheese. Place back into oven for 10-15 minutes, or until cheese is golden brown and bubbly. Drizzle with olive oil. Slice and place on a wire rack to cool. Serve with your favorite pizza sauce, as a side with soup or salad, or topped with spinach or arugula.

Emily R. Stone
GRILLED PITA BREAD GLUTEN-FREE

Ingredients:

1 package active dry yeast
1 cup warm water
3 cups gluten free all purpose flour
2 Tbsp olive oil
1 pinch of salt

Directions:

In a mixer bowl, add the yeast, warm water, and 1 cup of flour. Mix. Let stand for about 15 minutes, or until it gets foamy and bubbly. Add the olive oil and salt. Mix. Add the rest of the flour, a little at a time. Mix dough about 5 or 6 minutes, until it pulls away from the sides.

Lightly dust your hands, and then remove the dough ball from the bowl. Drizzle the bowl with olive oil. Add the dough back to the bowl, coating it with the olive oil. Cover with foil and let until the ball doubles in size, about 2 hours.

Remove the ball from the bowl and lay on a lightly dusted surface. Press flat to remove air. Cut dough into 8 equal slices. Roll each slice into a ball. Lightly cover with lightly greased plastic wrap. Let stand 30 minutes.

On a lightly floured surface, roll one ball into a 1/4 inch round. Let rest for 5 minutes. Cover the other dough balls with a towel. Place skillet over medium high heat. Oil the skillet. Place the pita bread inside and grill for about 3 minutes on each side. Bread should be golden browned and puffed. Continue until each ball is done. Serve as a wrap, miniature pizza dough, or fill the pocket with your favorite ingredients.

FALAFEL BALLS GLUTEN-FREE

Ingredients:

250 grams chickpeas (soaked overnight and drained twice)
4 garlic cloves
2 small carrots, grated
2 bunches fresh coriander
2 teaspoons salt
3 teaspoons cumin
Olive oil for frying
Buckwheat flour (optional)

Directions:

Place thoroughly drained chickpeas into a food processor. Add garlic, coriander, grated carrots, cumin, and salt. Mix. Drain or squeeze mixture until liquid is removed. Sprinkle the mixture with Buckwheat flour.

Place pan over medium heat. Add olive oil. Make small balls out of mixture. Fry on both sides until crunchy. Serve warm.

Emily R. Stone
SWEET POTATO LATKES GLUTEN-FREE

Ingredients:

1 large sweet potato, grated
1 egg
Salt to taste
Oil for frying

Directions:

Mix sweet potato, egg, and salt together in a bowl. Place pan over medium heat. Add oil. Drain potato mixture with side of spoon. Spoon mixture into the hot oil. Fry on both sides, until golden brown. Serve warm.

HUMMUS GLUTEN-FREE

Ingredients:

400 g chickpeas
1/4 cup Greek yogurt
1/4 cup tahini or tahini paste
1/4 tsp cumin
1 1/2 cup juice from a lemon
2 tsp olive oil
2 garlic cloves
Salt and pepper to taste

Directions:

Combine all ingredients into a food processor. Blend until smooth. Pour hummus into a serving dish. Serve with fresh vegetables or gluten-free pita chips.

Emily R. Stone
BAKED PITA CHIPS GLUTEN-FREE

Ingredients:

4 gluten-free pitas
Olive oil
Sea salt

Directions:

Preheat oven to 400 degrees. Cut pita bread into bite sized triangles. Place triangles flat on baking sheet. Brush with olive oil. Sprinkle with sea salt. Bake for 8-10 minutes. Serve with hummus.

STUFFED PITA POCKETS GLUTEN-FREE

Ingredients:

1 large tomato
1 cucumber
1 onion
1/2 cup kalamata olives
1/2 cup extra virgin olive oil
1 Tbsp oregano
Juice from 1/2 lemon
1 package Feta cheese
4 gluten-free pita pockets

Directions:

Chop tomato, cucumber, and onion, in a bowl. Add olives. Add feta cheese. Drizzle with olive oil. Add lemon juice and oregano. Toss. Slice pita bread in half. Fill each half with Greek salad. Serve.

Emily R. Stone
GREEK STYLE ROASTED POTATOES GLUTEN-FREE

Ingredients:

8 Russet potatoes peeled and cubed
1/4 cup lemon juice
1/2 cup olive oil
2 garlic cloves
1 Tbsp oregano
Salt and pepper to taste

Directions:

Add potatoes to salted, boiling water. Boil for 6 minutes. In a bowl add olive oil, lemon juice, garlic, oregano, and salt and pepper. Whisk together. Place potatoes into a bowl. Pour wet mixture on top of potatoes. Coat evenly.

Preheat oven to 400 degrees. Pour potatoes and mixture onto a parchment lined baking sheet. Bake for 40 minutes, turning half way through. Broil on low heat for last five minutes. Serve.

GRILLED LAMB CHOPS GLUTEN-FREE

Ingredients:

5 lamb chops
1/4 cup paprika
2 crushed garlic cloves
1/4 cup fresh mint, chopped
1 Tbsp cumin
1 tsp salt
2 Tbsp olive oil

Directions:

Place lamb chops in a bowl. Add mint, olive oil, paprika, cumin, salt, and garlic. Mix well. Cover and place in refrigerator overnight.

Place lamb chops on hot grill. Grill for about 3 minutes on each side, until meat is brown with grill sear marks. Serve with Tzatiki or your favorite dipping sauce.

Emily R. Stone
Tzatziki Gluten-Free

Ingredients:

1 cup Greek yogurt
1-2 tsp lemon juice
1 cucumber
1 tsp olive oil
2 garlic cloves
Salt and pepper to taste

Directions:

Grate cucumber then strain until all the liquid is gone. In a bowl, add yogurt, cucumber, olive oil, and lemon juice. Add garlic with a garlic press. Mix well. Add salt and pepper to taste. Serve with gluten free pita chips, raw vegetables, kebabs, or lamb chops.

CHAPTER EIGHT - 10
MEDITERRANEAN DIET SNACK/DESSERT RECIPES

SANGRIA GRANITA

Ingredients:

Oranges
¼ cup plus 2 Tbs. sugar (granulated)
¾ cup red wine (full-bodied -Cabernet or Merlot)
2 Tbs. fresh lemon juice
¼ cup fresh orange juice

Directions:

Combine the sugar, half cup of water and red wine in a mid-sized saucepan. Boil over medium heat for a minute. Mix in the lemon and orange juice. Let cool. Pour the mixture into a square shallow baking pan (9-inch). Cover with plastic and freeze over-night. Scrape up some shaved ice and fill chilled glasses or bowls.

Emily R. Stone

CREMA DI MASCARPONE (CHILLED CHEESE DESSERT)

Ingredients:

2 tbsp cognac (or other type of Brandy)
2 tbsp heavy cream
4 egg yolks (lightly beaten)
½ cup sugar
1 lb mascarpone (cream cheese or ricotta can be used)

Directions:

Use an electric blender to blend the cheese until consistency is smooth.

Beat in the cognac, cream, egg yolks and sugar until the mixture is very smooth and thick. Refrigerate till well-chilled.

BERLINGOZZO

Ingredients:

A pinch of salt
1½ cups milk
1 tbsp baking powder
Zest of 1 lemon
3½ oz. melted butter
3 cups flour
2 egg yolks
1 cup sugar
2eggs

Directions:

Use electric mixer to beat eggs and sugar until mixture is pale yellow. Add flour, melted butter, lemon zest, pinch of salt and mix by hand.

Add milk and stir until batter is smooth.

Add baking powder and continue mixing batter. Pour batter into buttered and floured cake tin. Bake in oven at 350 degrees for 30-40 minutes. Cake top should be golden brown when done.

Emily R. Stone

HONEY AND TAHINI GANACHE WITH TOASTED SESAME SEEDS

Ingredients:

¾ cup sesame seeds
12-1/2 oz. Caribbean 66% chopped dark chocolate
⅓ cup Tahini
2-1/2 Tbs. heather honey or strong clover

Directions:

Bring honey and three quarter cup water to a simmer. Put in the tahini and let simmer for two minutes. After, pour the hot liquid on the chocolate and combine until smooth. Let cool. Refrigerate to allow ganache to set.

Toast sesame seeds lightly in a frying pan with no oil. Add ganache and roll them through sesame seeds. Serve at room temperature.

POACHED CHERRIES

Ingredients:

⅔ cup sugar
4 strips lemon zest, 1x2 inches each
⅛ split vanilla beans
14 peppercorns
1 pound fresh pitted, sweet cherries

Directions:

Bring sugar, water, citrus zest, peppercorn and vanilla bean to a boil. Keep stirring until the sugar dissolves. Add cherries and let simmer about 10 minutes. Skim foam off of the top, let mixture cool and then refrigerate. Strain poaching liquid before serving.

Emily R. Stone
Berry Panna Cotta

Ingredients:

2 cups fresh berries
Pinch salt
1 tablespoon sugar
⅓ cup honey
3 cups whipping cream
1 tbsp powdered gelatin (unflavored)
1 cup whole milk

Directions:

Put the milk in a tiny bowl and sprinkle in the gelatin. Allow to stand for no more than five minutes. Pour the mixture into saucepan and mix over medium flame until the gelatin is fully dissolved but do not allow milk to boil. Add the salt, sugar, honey and cream. Mix until the sugar dissolves. Half fill six wine glasses. Refrigerate 6 hours. Put the berries on the panna cotta before serving.

ROASTED FIGS WITH CARAMEL

Ingredients:

Ricotta cheese
1/2 cup Granulated sugar
12 firm ripe figs
Whipped cream or ricotta cheese for garnish

Directions:

Heat the oven to 450°F. Stand figs upright in baking dish. Spread sugar evenly in skillet on medium-low heat. Let cook until sugar turns honey color. Pour caramel over figs. Roast figs in caramel for 15 minutes. Cool figs in fridge. Drizzle caramel over figs, and garnish with whipped cream or ricotta.

Emily R. Stone
RED GRAPE, POLENTA & OLIVE OIL CAKE

Ingredients:

Confectioners' sugar
1-3/4 cups seedless grapes (red)
1 tsp. grated lemon zest
1 tsp. pure vanilla extract
⅓ cup milk
½ cup extra-virgin olive oil
⅔ cup granulated sugar
2 large eggs
¼ tsp. table salt
1-1/2 tsp. baking powder
½ cup yellow cornmeal
1 cup all-purpose flour (unbleached)

Directions:

Preheat oven to 350ºF. Mix salt, baking powder, cornmeal and flour in a bowl. Combine sugar and eggs in large bowl. Add oil in slowly and mix at medium speed for about a minute. Mix in lemon zest, vanilla, milk and flour mixture half cup at a time and half of the grapes. Place batter into 9 inch pan and let bake for ten minutes. Add remaining grapes and bake about forty minutes. Dust with confectioners' sugar then cut it in wedges before serving.

AINSE & FIG ICE CREAM

Ingredients:

1 cup crème fraîche
3 large eggs (separated)
1 tsp. aniseed
⅓ cup honey
2 cups half and half or cream
⅓ cup plus 2 Tbs. sugar
1-1/2 lb. ripe figs (unpeeled with the stems removed)

Directions:

Purée the figs. Transfer to a skillet (10-inch) with a third cup of the sugar and let cook over medium heat for 30 minutes. Boil aniseed, honey and cream in a saucepan over medium heat. To the egg yolks add the hot cream and whisk. Put on low heat to cook until mixture thickens. Transfer to bowl. Mix in the crème fraîche and fig purée and chill. Whisk the egg whites until foamy and add remaining sugar. Fold the egg whites into the fig purée, and then put in an ice-cream maker to freeze.

Emily R. Stone
RED WINE POACHED PEAR

Ingredients:

2 teaspoons of cinnamon
2 teaspoons vanilla
2 Tablespoons of lemon juice (lemon zest can be added)
¾ cups of sugar (granulated)
1½ cups of red wine (Merlot, Shiraz or Zinfandel)
4-6 Pears (peeled, cored and sliced)-(Anjou or Bosc)

Directions:

Mix all the ingredients, excluding the pears, and let come to a boil. Turn heat to a simmer and put in the pears. Let pears simmer for no more than twelve minutes then turn pears and let simmer for another ten minutes. Take the pears out and allow them to cool. Let wine sauce boil until liquid is cut down by half. Pour the sauce over the pears and then serve with Devonshire cream, crème fraiche or mascarpone.

ABOUT THE AUTHOR

Emily R. Stone loves to eat, but really does not like the added pounds that can be gained. As a result, she has spent a great deal of time trying to find recipes that not only taste great, but that will keep her from gaining weight. When she was introduced to the Mediterranean Diet, she appreciated the fact that she could eat a large variety of fresh, delicious and healthy foods without the worry.

Ms. Stone also loves sharing her knowledge and experience with others who may be searching for ways to eat healthier. So, she dove into her recipe box and gathered 50 of her most favorite Mediterranean diet recipes. Enjoy!

CPSIA information can be obtained
at www.ICGtesting.com
Printed in the USA
LVHW070450231120
672386LV00001B/6

9 781630 228910